T0247659

*A Riderless Horse*

# A Riderless Horse
*Tim Upperton*

AUCKLAND
UNIVERSITY
PRESS

First published 2022
Auckland University Press
University of Auckland
Private Bag 92019
Auckland 1142
New Zealand
www.aucklanduniversitypress.co.nz

ISBN 978 1 86940 977 7

Earle Creativity and Development Trust
in Manawatū and Rangitikei

A catalogue record for this book is available from
the National Library of New Zealand

Book and cover design by Duncan Munro

This book was printed on FSC® certified paper
Printed in Singapore by Markono Print Media Pte Ltd

*For Oscar, Tess, Ben and Katrina*

# Contents

# My childhood

I was Dick. I teased Anne and George.
I was Edmund, betrayed my friends
for a sweet. Something rotten in me.
Cast out, castaway. For long years
I had an island to myself.
I lived on corn, goat meat, fish. All changed
by a single footprint in the sand.
I harkened to the call of the wild.
The trees cracked in the cold.
How lost, how alone I was. I howled.
I hunted. I ate. My bloodied muzzle.
I left that place and took rooms
in foggy London. I solved the case
of the speckled band. Then I split in two.
I avoided mirrors. My other self
was murderous, but I grew kinder.
In the end I lost everything.
Take my eyes, I said to a swallow.
He flew with them across the city.

# YRROS

You had done a bad thing.
You knew you had to apologise.

I, who have done bad things
always and had to apologise

for another and yet another, said,
You must say sorry.

Long ago, after another said,
You must say sorry,

I said, No.
But I knew I had to.

You knew you couldn't say, No.
You knew you had to

say sorry, but you said it backwards.
You bore your apology like a cross,

defiantly. Said backwards
it became a sound an ocean bird, an albatross,

might make, a lonely cry above
the murmuring sea.

I heard a word in your cry, above
the murmuring sea,

a word not said rightly,
a word I should know.

The wrong life cannot be lived rightly.
I should know.

There is time and time to apologise.
Still, ahead of you, the bad thing.

# True story

*for Ruth Upperton, 1931–2013*

It was 1936, my mother was five years old.
Her mother had given her a china doll.
Her sister, aged four, had been given one too.

The dolls were beautiful, with print cotton dresses
and chubby arms and legs and clear faces
and such blue eyes and fine, golden hair.

Story goes my mother dropped hers
on the cracked path that led from the gate
to the old bungalow—

new then, the only house on the street
that still had a chimney after the earthquake
the year my mother was born—

and anyway the doll broke and that was that.
My mother turned to her sister, my aunt,
and stared at her in pain. Her sister stared back.

The blazing sun poured down.
It was long ago. Two old ladies chuckling
with each other, remembering.

And then my mother snatched her sister's doll
from her hands and smashed it on the ground.
I am the only one who knows this story.

# In Topeka, Kansas

Well, after all, you want to be free.
You want to wear a faded tee shirt

with a hole in the armpit, of a weekend,
to fetch up in Topeka, Kansas,

and to have a wife who's pleasant in her ways,
some rowdy kids, a tipped-over

bicycle in the yard and a rose garden—
big, showy yellow roses—

out front that your venerable neighbours
admire, in their courtly fashion, as they pass.

That's how it is in Topeka, you imagine,
that's how it is, but already you're fretful,

the yellow roses a step too far, and besides,
the old threads are looping around again,

tying you into the wicker chair on the porch
where you sit and swat the flies away,

the flies being so bothersome in summer,
in Topeka, Kansas, all the livelong day.

# Love poem

My load, my lode,
my burden, my treasure,
you are so heavy!
How long
must I carry you?
Forever?
Very well then—
I will carry you
forever.

# Grace

All these people had come to an outdoor fair.
They were walking from one stall
to another, inspecting the goods for sale,

picking up a jar of quince jelly
and holding it to the light,
tipping it sideways to test the set,

putting it down again.
Everyone was eating instant noodles
from disposable cups. In one hand

they held the cup, and in the other
they held the sachet of flavouring
and a plastic fork. They were trying

to sprinkle the flavouring on their noodles,
but what with walking around
and the fork and a light breeze blowing,

most of the dry powder drifted away
or fell to the ground.
One man tore his sachet and shook it furiously,

spilling its contents everywhere. I'd had enough.
'Stop!' I shouted to the crowd,
and a few looked my way.

'You're losing the flavouring! Make a funnel'—
I waved the paper serviette that came with the noodles—
'with this!' I quickly made a funnel,

poured the flavouring on to the noodles.
None was wasted!
More people gathered around.

Some fumbled with their flavour sachets,
made funnels with their serviettes,
but they made them wrong,

and the flavouring missed their cups.
I was losing them. They dispersed,
diverted by the many other attractions,

leaving a fine yellow cloud of noodle flavouring
in the now still air, like pollen,
like grace so available nobody wanted it.

# Mayfly

Maybe it was the lone trout fisherman
I saw yesterday, as I drove over
the bridge, his fly rod a thin wand, almost
invisible at dusk—all night I dreamed

of mayflies, swarming bright around my head
like a saint's inconvenient halo.
The mayfly has no functioning mouthparts—
its plans are necessarily short-term.

From my bed I can make out my mother's
old high-back chair, the dim bookshelves, faceless
framed photographs, window, starlight. No moon.
Where did all my dear ones go, where are they

now? I'm not sure about the mouthparts, could
check it out online, but I feel better
not knowing. In the sleeping house I clump
downstairs and in the kitchen I thank God,

as I gulp down some cereal, I have
functioning mouthparts, and for my other
excellent parts I am also grateful,
and isn't the mayfly's dance, like this poem

I'm writing in the dark, a spell against
death? Not a very good spell, obviously.
Least profitable enterprise ever,
after poetry: mayfly life insurance.

Does the mayfly think like this? You can bet
as it swarms, as it mates, lays eggs and dies,
it's thinking, How the fuck did I get here?
Why didn't I just stay in the cool stream?

Nymph-life was so good! To eat and grow fat—
God, what I'd give to do that all again!
To which I say, Embrace life! No regrets!
Isn't the upper air the clearest thing

you could ever imagine? Who'd have thought
you could ever move like this, feel like this?
And now dawn comes, with its rosy fingers,
the house creaks and wakes, but I'm not finished!

Maybe the fallen mayfly thinks that, too,
its body a scribble writ in water.
I'm not finished! Its wings heavier now,
tiny, swaddled Ophelia. I'm finished.

# Lunch on the grass

It was pleasant on the grass. We were just sitting around. The wine in the glasses was pale green. There was a woman beside me. She was very attractive to me, but I was distracted by the presence of a small, shiny blue-green beetle of some kind on her bare thigh, quite motionless. Such a tiny beetle, on that vast plain! That's the sort of day it was. 'Try the potato salad!' the woman said. 'If you don't try the potato salad, I shall die!' 'I don't like potato salad,' I said. I spoke more stiffly than the occasion warranted. She looked at me sadly, and sank into the grass. I, too, felt a deep sadness. All my life I have made enemies, despite my best intentions. I looked away, wishing I were somewhere else. The other picnic-goers were, I sensed, turning against me. A rustling sound came from the leaves of the hedge, or perhaps from a small animal deep within the hedge, perhaps a mouse. I could feel the mouse's feelings, wanting, as I did, a place of concealment. 'Try the potato salad!' remonstrated the bearded man reclining opposite me. He was wearing some sort of frock-coat. 'Yes, try the potato salad!' everyone said in unison. 'But I don't like potato salad,' I said, and you can guess what happened next.

# The end of my driveway
*after a series of photographs by Edith Amituanai*

At the end of my driveway the world begins.
At the end of my driveway the world is going.

Kids drift past trees and recycling bins.
Kids wander by, their faces glowing.

In summer sun and winter storms
kids walk to school in their uniforms.

Inside their uniforms, their itching skins.
Inside their skins, the kids are growing.

This girl frowns, this boy ducks his head and grins:
not yet seeing, not yet knowing

that what's gone is a new beginning,
that what begins is already going

fast then faster. Adults, with their set faces,
whoosh by in cars to adult places.

# School caretaker

I get up at dawn. One of those early wakers.
At the school by six, I work unseen,
which is how I like it. What I make is

soon unmade. I guess my mistake is
I take care. The grounds so neat, tidy, and green.
But here they come, the troublemakers.

They trample all over my fine green acres.
The enamel in the toilets gleams. It's clean.
But not for long. Not with these jokers.

I come from a long line of caretakers.
The kids are all right. They're OK. I mean,
when I forget where the spade or the rake is,

they'll find it for me. On my birthday, a cake is
presented by the food tech class in the school canteen.
It's sometimes a flop, but I thank the bakers.

And the cake has green icing, and for my sake a
tiny lawnmower, and a tiny seated figurine
a bit like me, with its tiny cap, its red windbreaker.
They know I care. I'm the school caretaker.

# Manawatū

The river twists like an eel
that twists within the twist

that is the river. The eel is a tube
that carries the river within it,

like the pipe that carries within it
what it pours into the river.

What pours all day into the river
becomes the river, as the child

who swims all day in the river
becomes a river-child,

and goes home in the evening
smelling of the river. The child

who swims in the river
dreams in the night of the river,

brown, flowing to the sea
with a burden it must disgorge,

and in that flow the flash
of the eel's upturned belly,

and the child, and everyone
the child has ever known,

faces upturned too and pale
in the moonlight, in the river,

so many faces, always more,
floating down the river

to where the river is going,
to where it widens, to the sea.

# Nobody knows

Many things make me sad these days,
the days make me sad, how they fade
into night so soon, how today
becomes yesterday, and then
last year, then seven years ago
when my mother died. She never
minded the passing of time,
getting old. Such a beauty she was.
Divorcing at seventy was a surprise.
She used to sing, sometimes, in a high voice,
'Nobody knows—the troubles I've seen,'
and towards the end she'd sing,
'Nobody knows . . .' and then trail away,
and we knew and didn't know.

# Sparrows

Seven plump sparrows pecking
at something in the grass—
they were having such a good time,
obviously. They were going for it,
and right then the best thing
would've been to be an eighth sparrow,
pecking at the ground with my friends,
eating I don't know what—seeds?
I'm thinking to myself, this is the life!
Wind's getting up a little, but let me tell you:
these seeds are great. Just great.
I'm chucking them down, the sun
on my back, earth steady beneath
my clawed feet, and high in a tree a nest
I built myself and a mate to return to.

# The truth about Palmerston North

*after James Brown*

People like to mock my town,
they mock it for being too provincial
and too boring, and it's true

that not much of import happens here
but I like it. Some people say
when they are asked what they like

about Palmerston North
that you can always find a park
and that's true, too, you can always find a park

just a short walk from where you want to go,
sometimes right outside,
you don't have to walk at all, you're right there.

Of course it's mostly only people
who live in New Zealand who mock
Palmerston North, as people who live

outside New Zealand know nothing about it.
People who don't live in New Zealand mock
our entire little country as a 1950s

throwback with honest, rural folk
and unspoilt scenery, which isn't quite true—
our scenery is spoilt from being looked at

too often and freedom campers, they say,
are a problem, but me, I blame dairy cows.
When I lived in the UK people there

thought New Zealand was a state of Australia,
and they would ask me what was coming up
on *Neighbours*, thinking I had some kind

of inside knowledge, but the truth is
I don't even watch *Neighbours* or indeed
any soap operas. Actually the whole

Southern Hemisphere is more or less
written off by people who don't live
in this part of the world, as somewhere

insignificant, like Palmerston North,
where as I said nothing much happens.
And it's an undeniable fact that the magazines

I subscribe to come from exotic places
that they flaunt in their titles, magazines
like *The New Yorker* and *London Review of Books*

and *The Paris Review*
but not *The Palmerston Northerner*.
It's another fact that *The Paris Review*

isn't even published in Paris
and has nothing to say about that city
but it has insightful interviews

with famous writers, some of whom
I have read. I have been to Paris
and apart from the architecture

and the food and some very fine cemeteries
and of course the language
it's quite like Palmerston North,

though parking is a nightmare.
I never visited the Louvre
but one fine afternoon

I went to the Musée d'Orsay,
which in the opinion of many educated people
really is just as good if you like Impressionist

and Post-Impressionist art, which I do.
Still it was nice to come home again,
home to Palmerston North, New Zealand,

and to see the good brown Manawatū River
moving sluggishly under the bridge.
It's not the Seine, but water is water.

Paul Celan threw himself—odd phrase,
as if he were both baseball and pitcher—
into the Seine. John Cleese said

Palmerston North is the suicide capital
of New Zealand, yet you don't hear of people
throwing themselves into the Manawatū,

which would be a risky business,
but only because of the effluent
from those dairy cows leaching into the river.

We live on a floodplain,
and the river is ever in our thoughts
and sometimes our houses.

At such times we are downcast,
but we raise our eyes unto the hills
and the windmills perched on them

that turn and turn.
It was in the Plaza, our spacious shopping mall,
that I saw a middle-aged woman

with her head tilted to where the sky
would have been, but for the ceiling
and the mood lighting,

a stout middle-aged woman
with black mascara, elegantly dressed,
her wet mouth a dark, soundless O,

and the crowd not unsympathetically parting
and reforming around her—rock in the river—
noticing and not noticing, which is our way.

# Sizewell A and B

In the photo of the beach at Aldeburgh,
the brightly painted fishing boats

are pulled up high on the shingle,
beneath a leaden sky. I had turned

to exclude the nuclear power stations,
Sizewell A and B, from the frame.

They were not what I wanted—
I wanted the nineteenth century,

the irrecoverable past,
the fishing boats, the gulls wheeling

and dipping, whitecaps
on the grey water.

You are also outside the frame,
striding and stumbling along

the beach, your green coat
flapping around your legs.

If I could return,
I would take the picture differently,

and invite in the power stations,
and their towers, as belonging

to that place, and you,
your face flushed with effort.

All I ever turned my back on,
I'd welcome in—

                 and here you are, at last,
struggling through the loose shingle

of that long ago decade, when happiness
wheeled all about us, struggling

towards me, forgetful me,
improbably in the picture too.

# Wild bees

*after James K. Baxter and D. H. Lawrence*

Got home in my car
and a bad mood
with a boxful of groceries

and the bees were everywhere
at once, zinging
around the wooden porch.

I was stung twice getting in the door.
I peered out the window.
The bees looked small and black and mean.

Of course I love bees!
Without bees, the planet's fucked, right?
Who doesn't love bees!

I filled a bucket, took it outside,
flung the water at them.
I was stung twice again.

Back in the house
I could feel a vibration
in the doorframe.

There was a gap between wall
and ceiling, and two or three bees
were crawling out.

My house is not a planet,
it is my house,
and these bees, I did not love them.

When I was two years old
I was stung by a bee
on my foot and my mother said

my entire leg swelled
and turned black.
It turned black!

I nearly died.
Did I, though? Maybe it's just one
of my mother's stories.

I got the fly spray
and sprayed in the gap.
Nothing. I sprayed some more.

Then a deep, angry murmur
from inside the wall.
Several more bees stumbled out.

I sprayed again.
I sprayed the entire can,
and stuffed a tea-towel into the gap.

The murmur grew louder,
a dull collective groan,
then died away.

It wasn't Carthage sacked,
or Troy, or anything like that.
Nor had I missed my chance

with any lords of life.
I have nothing to expiate.
I cannot share my house with bees.

There's plenty of nature outside,
glades and such,
where I may encounter bees,

and perhaps other creatures,
and commune with them,
and enjoy spiritual experiences.

Outside! My house is not a glade!
My house is my house, where I live.
It is not a meadow!

# Game show

Contestants are awarded points for cooperation and goodwill. Their kindness flows like unstoppable sweet porridge. The conch-blower hands the conch over to a guy who hasn't blown it in a while, and the top contestant shyly gives her points away to the one coming last. There is no prize, except perhaps a word, a nod, a look from the game show host, who is kindest of all.

I settle in each week to see how they're all doing. The tanned young man has undone his bandanna and tied it around the tough old woman's knee. It's just a graze from the coral, but you can't be too careful. She gives him a fish she speared. He gives her a worn copy of *Jonathan Livingston Seagull*. He's vegetarian, she's a literature professor, and you know he won't eat the fish and she won't read the book. Their gratitude towards each other shines so bright I have to look away.

Each week more and more people are voted on to the island, until their numbers are too great for the widescreen TV to hold. The final episode is just one epic good deed after another, everyone egging each other on. I'm egging them on too, from the couch. The show is not popular, but its modest audience is increasing. A second season is in the works.

# Television

Inside the television the tiny people
are moving and talking. Some of them

are falling in love. Some of them are dying
in exciting ways. The cartoon people

who fall off a cliff or are hit by a train
get up again, scowling but unharmed.

There are also tiny animals.
They live in documentaries.

They hunt and fall in love and die.
They do not get up again.

At night the television is turned off
and all the people and all the animals

lie down and go to sleep.
The people sleep in tiny houses.

The animals sleep in and under tiny trees.
It is crowded inside the television,

but they are all used to it
and they make do. They settle down

under their tiny night sky,
with its tiny stars.

Who would not wish
to join them there?

A young woman with wet hair
climbs out of the television

into a living room,
her long hair and sodden dress

are dripping water on the floor,
and that is a horror movie.

But more and more of us
are going into the television,

and the young woman will soon
be alone in the world.

She wanders from empty house
to empty house, testing the abandoned

appliances. She picks up the remote
and switches the television on,

but then she is bored
and switches it off.

There is nothing to be afraid of
inside the television. It's quite all right.

Good night, we tiny people
say to each other.

Good night, the tiny animals
growl and squeak and purr.

The television is dark now.
Good night.

# The Kingdom of Suck Balls Mountain
*Barry*, Season 2, Episode 3

When Akhmal the inept Chechen hitman
is himself hit, and NoHo Hank
kicks his wounded arm and says,

'You suck balls!'—
which is unkind at such a time—
and Akhmal screeches in pain

and shouts, 'And you're the King
of Suck Balls Mountain!'
                    —you have to wonder

about the Kingdom of Suck Balls Mountain,
and its castle near the mist-shrouded peak,
with its crenellated battlements,

from which you look out, on a fine day,
over Eat Shit Plain, bordered by the shining
Wouldn't Piss On You If You Were On Fire River.

Incompetency is the rule there
and government officials wear bright, ill-fitting
uniforms with brass buttons and truth be told

it's not so great, as kingdoms go,
but it beats the neighbouring kingdoms of Kiss My Ass
and That's Not What Your Mother Said,

and see how the sun burnishes the ripe barley
in the field! The wagons on the dusty roads
are fully laden, the mistle thrush pipes its song

from the wood, and NoHo Hank
has begun a shuffling kind of jig
and Akhmal, being Chechen and all,

can't help but get to his feet and join him,
clutching his wounded arm,
and the Kingdom of Suck Balls Mountain

is maybe not where you wanted to end up,
maybe not where you would wish to be a citizen,
but as you take Akhmal's hand tenderly,

so as not to hurt his arm, it's where you are,
everyone is somewhere,
like Akhmal, wounded and dancing.

# Bone

The man is tired of digging.
The shovel is tired of the ground.
The ground resents the shovel,
and is tired of the weight
of the man standing above.

How long has he stood there,
in the wind and the rain?
Isn't he cold? Surely he is cold.
It is time for the man to lie down
in the ground.

The man is not tired then.
The man rests. The shovel rests
on its mound, with its concave face
turned to the sky. The ground
also rests. Bone is what is left.

Bone is what carried the flesh
until it tired of carrying
and lay down.
Then the flesh departed,
and bone was by itself.

The ground became dust
and blew away.
Bone remembered the flesh
and missed its warmth,
its softness, its weight.

Bone lay white beneath the moon.
The wind blew, and bone shivered
against bone, clattered a little,
like a chime.
Came a whistling sound.

# Small griefs

The way dead leaves
          thicken
               at the bottom of a treed slope—
                    even when the trees are ever-
                      green, even on a gentle slope

# Three men in a lift

is what we were, three men in a lift
at a conference on coffee break
and the lift jammed—nothing serious,

we knew that, we were on the first floor
and it wasn't going anywhere—
and we got talking, as you do,

to pass the time, and I told these men
how when I was little my father
killed somebody, like on purpose,

he went to jail for a long time,
and how it fucks you up,
having a killer for a dad,

how you are isolated from others
by the fact of it,
how you isolate yourself,

how you wonder sometimes,
if you've got it, the killer gene.
I get angry now and then—

not angry like my dad,
but angry slamming doors,
smashing things, expensive things,

and later making amends,
flowers, cards, the whole sorry mess.
Well the other two men were silent

for a bit while the lift lurched and made
a complicated graunching sound,
then the short man with white stubble

on his cheeks—he had a white shirt
a little yellow around the collar,
a conference pen in the pocket—

he cleared his throat and said his father
was also a killer. First the family dog,
he strangled it with its own leash

for barking maybe, or did it piss
on the carpet? And then a fight
with the man next door, something

about fresh washing on the line,
drifting barbecue smoke,
and bang went the neighbour's head

on the concrete driveway and wham,
jail, four years. It sure changes you,
the short man said, loosening his tie.

It sure does, said the third man,
who until this point hadn't said a word,
had just eyed the lift ceiling from time

to time as if it might offer a suggestion,
a way out of our common predicament.
His father, too, had killed somebody—

his mother when he was a baby.
He didn't remember it of course,
everyone said it was the damnedest thing.

His father had pushed her off a balcony.
The few times his dad spoke of it,
the third man said, it was like he'd knocked

a potted cyclamen off a shelf.
This man was bald and pale,
in the lift's fluorescent light,

unlined and soft, like a baby still,
as if he'd stopped aging about the time
his mother stopped aging,

that is to say, got killed by his father.
That poor woman, he said,
tears running down his face,

I never knew her.
What are the odds? I said
to these two men,

raising my hands, I admit it,
a little theatrically.
What are the odds,

the three of us
stuck here in this lift,
and all with killer dads?

We shook our heads.
It was a pure moment
of companionable sorrow,

and the lift gave another lurch,
a jolt, one that meant business
this time, and the lift doors slid open,

and waiting in the lobby was a cluster
of conference attendees, all men,
just standing there gawping—

they must've been impatient for the lift,
they were practically leaning on the doors,
sudden tang of sweat and deodorant—

what had they heard? The lift huffed
an exhausted sigh for all of us. Yeah, I said
loudly, to the pack of waiting men,

like your dads never killed anybody,
and I ducked my head and I pushed,
I pushed my way through.

# Space

The space between Earth and Mars
is the space between two worlds.
It is the space between two words.
Earth calls out to Mars, but Mars
slowly turns away.
Earth calls out again.
Hey Mars! But there is no one
on Mars to hear. Earth sends people
to Mars. When the people arrive
at the silent, empty world,
there is great excitement.
Earth calls out, Hey Mars!
Mars calls back, Hey Earth!
And each world is glad
to be less alone.

# Moon

I never see a man's face.
I see a rabbit sometimes,
its ears up, running, I guess,
but where? It's on the moon,
where there is no grass,
no atmosphere, no air to breathe.
Hardly any gravity,
so in its short life it leaps
higher than any earthly rabbit,
weightlessly it bounds
across that empty space,
bounds and bounds again,
with never a burrow.

# Green monkey soap

Best toy I ever had was my green monkey soap. It wasn't really a toy, not like a soft toy. It had no fur, no stuffing on the inside. It had no glass eyes. It didn't even have arms and legs, or a tail. Its physical details were bumps and indentations in the soap, which flaked and chipped over the course of that year, the year of the green monkey soap. Its features blurred, and towards the end it didn't look like a monkey at all. It was just a small lump of green soap, and finally its soapy scent was gone, but still I held it in my hand and whispered to it in the dark. I never played with my green monkey soap, it was more of a steadfast companion. Damn I miss that monkey.

# Dead pets

Nipper and Whiskers, Wuff and Wag,
where did they go? Wuff 'went to a farm'.
Wag went under a car. Whiskers was buried in a bag.
Nipper simply disappeared. I cried buckets. Calm

down, my dad said. Calm the fuck down.
And not knowing what else to do, tired of crying
for my little cat Nipper somewhere dying,
I calmed the fuck down.

# The riderless horses

One evening that summer a riderless horse galloped along our road, empty stirrups slapping. We ran up the driveway screaming to our mother. Quick, inside! she said. She shut and locked the door, closed the windows. The horse tried the door handle, its large eye pressed to the keyhole. It prowled around the house. The fume of its breath misted the windows. It couldn't get in! We laughed with relief. My brother remembers it differently, when I call him up, but we agree on the rattle of the door handle. Stupid Mum! I say to the dog. He chews on a dried pig's ear—I bought him a packet of them at the supermarket. Boy loves to chew. I pull another ear from the packet and whisper into it, *I'm sorry, I'm sorry*, but it's heard it all before. It's getting late. I hear the beat of hooves, and from every direction the riderless horses come.

# Door

I hear a knock at the door,
but I am busy, I have a lot to do,
a lot to think about.

The world outside will have to wait.
What does it matter to me
if a couple sit on a blanket

in the park across the street,
if yellow leaves are falling?
Again, someone knocking,

louder this time. This is not new,
I have heard the knocking
many times

for what might be months, years,
sometimes soft, almost a touch,
a caress, sometimes a peremptory tap,

sometimes frantic banging and shouting.
It's all the same, I am working,
I will not be disturbed.

Peaches moulder in the blue china bowl.
The house is silent now.
How long have I been sitting here

as the shadows lengthen?
When did I last hear anything,
anything at all?

This quiet that is also a disquiet
presses upon me,
and I do an unusual thing,

I get up from my chair, I go to the door.
I turn the handle,
and the door swings inwards.

In the doorway, fitted to the frame,
is another closed door.
One with no handle.

Who would build such a thing,
without my knowledge?
Who would do this to me?

I have harmed no one.
I give the door a push,
but it doesn't move.

I knock, and wait,
but nobody answers.
I knock harder.

# Cough

Not long ago I had a cough. A nagging cough.
I'd wake up with it in the night. Christ! Cough cough cough.
Of course it got better. It was only a cough.
One day I realised an hour had passed—no cough.
I know some other day it'll come back, the cough,
or something like it. It'll get worse. It'll say, enough.

# Roadside trees

Just as the ants in their dark troop will touch
muzzle to muzzle—as they ask the way,
perhaps, or how the day goes—it was such

with these, who, ending their brief interplay,
continued on their solitary paths,
had somewhere to be, and all the long day

to get through, bodies itching in their clothes,
the coffee break, the lunch eaten alone,
and in the cold evening air their breaths

suspended above their heads like cartoon
speech bubbles yet to be captioned, the words
elusive, making a silence someone

might fill, as the roadside trees darken. Birds'
cries subside, a car engine coughs, backfires.
Home, a glass of wine, a second, a third,

pizza delivered, TV. The slow hours
pass. Trudge to the bathroom, brush, spit and floss,
squint in the mirror, run a warm shower.

What was it you waited for? Was it this?
You lie in bed, blinking at the ceiling.
What was never quite yours you lately miss,

a tune your mother would hum while dealing
cards, four of you at the dining table,
or three and a dummy hand, that feeling

you had no name for then, impossible
it couldn't last, impossible it could.
The *Reader's Digest*, a cracked brown bible,

Zane Grey westerns, an atlas of the world—
your father would point and say, you are here.
Tonight you feel lost, as in a dark wood:

here is not what you wanted, or hoped for.
Hard truth is that you never asked for much,
and got less. How far still to go, how far.

# Writ on the eve of my 53rd birthday

*after Gregory Corso*


Once I was very small but then I grew up
and other things were small and nothing hurt
like it did when I was sixteen, and again
at twenty-one. Fifty-fucking-three!

The poems I wrote and the poems I shouldn't
have written but they're done now and in books
nobody, absolutely nobody,
ever reads. There was some craziness,

and sometimes I was alone and other times
I was not alone, and alone was better
but I was lonely. To be honest,
the craziness didn't amount to much.

The confessional stopped working about
the time I had things to confess, and now—
now I'd have to spend the rest of my life
in there and still never get to the end

of it, fuck it, I may as well carry on.
My hair was long and straight but went springy
in my thirties then straight again but not
as straight as before. Now it's mostly grey

but I don't really care about it.
I let it grow and grow and then I cut
it all off. I imagine it growing
when I'm lifeless in my coffin, masses

of it, which is unpleasant to think of
and anyway not yet. I want more life
in front of me than I have behind me,
but that's not about to happen. I want

a bell I could ring, in the wormy darkness,
like in the Edgar Allan Poe story—
I could pull the string, ting-a-ling, and please
be there, somebody above, just in case.

# Homecoming

It is a long way from here,
but there is a map.

It is in another country,
but we have passports and visas,

and I speak the language.
The people are friendly,

or if not friendly, they know me
and they will not harm you.

There is no map,
but I know the way,

and even in bad weather, when roads
are sometimes impassable,

there are inexpensive inns
where we can spend the night.

The currency is strange there,
but these are my people,

and when you are among my people
you won't need money,

they will take care of you,
they will treat you like family.

My family left the village long ago.
They are all dead now,

they died in wars no one
speaks of anymore,

but still the people there
remember them.

'It's you!' they will say
when we get there.

'We knew you would come.
Welcome home.'

# Notes

'YRROS' includes a line, 'The wrong life cannot be lived
rightly', which is lifted from Theodor Adorno's *Minima
Moralia* (New Left Books, 1974).

'Lunch on the grass' is an ekphrastic poem on Édouard
Manet's painting, *Le déjeuner sur l'herbe*.

'The end of my driveway' was commissioned by the *School
Journal* to accompany an article on the photography of
Edith Amituanai.

'School caretaker' was commissioned for the children's poetry
anthology, *Skinny Dip* (Annual Ink, 2021).

'The truth about Palmerston North' is indebted to the poem
'I come from Palmerston North', by James Brown.

'Manawatū' was commissioned by Te Manawa for the 'Black
River' exhibition, a collaboration between poets and
printmakers in 2015.

'Wild bees' is after James K. Baxter's 'Wild bees' and
D. H. Lawrence's 'Snake'.

'Roadside trees' was commissioned for an anthology
commemorating the 700th anniversary of Dante's death,
*More Favourable Waters* (The Cuba Press, 2021). The first
stanza is from Clive James's translation of the *Purgatorio*
(Picador, 2013).

'Writ on the eve of my 53rd birthday' is after Gregory Corso's
'Writ on the Eve of My 32nd Birthday'.

# Acknowledgements

Most of these poems have been previously published, often in different versions, in *Best New Zealand Poems*, *Black River: A Collaboration in Print and Poetry*, *Landfall*, *More Favourable Waters*, *NZ Poetry Shelf*, *Poetry*, *School Journal*, *Skinny Dip*, *Sport*, *The Spinoff*, *takahē* and *Turbine | Kapohau*. My thanks to the editors and curators.

Thanks also to Creative New Zealand and the Earle Creativity Trust who awarded me grants to complete this book, and to the Caselberg Trust who awarded me the Caselberg Trust International Poetry Prize in 2020.

I've had help from lots of people with these poems. I'd especially like to thank Bryan Walpert, Kim Worthington, Nick Ascroft, and the Red Pen Writers Group for encouragement, feedback and suggestions.

Thanks most of all to my children, Oscar, Tess, Ben and Katrina. What stars you are.

**Tim Upperton** lives in Palmerston North. He has published two previous poetry collections, *A House on Fire* (Steele Roberts, 2009) and *The Night We Ate the Baby* (HauNui Press, 2014), which was a finalist in the Ockham New Zealand Book Awards. He won the Bronwyn Tate Memorial International Poetry Competition in 2011 and the Caselberg International Poetry Competition in 2012, 2013 and 2020. His poems have been widely published in magazines including *Agni*, *Poetry*, *Shenandoah*, *Sport*, *takahē* and *Landfall*, and are anthologised in *The Best of Best New Zealand Poems* (Victoria University Press, 2011), *Villanelles* (Everyman's Library, 2012), *Essential New Zealand Poems* (Random House, 2014), *Obsession: Sestinas in the Twenty-First Century* (Dartmouth College Press, 2014), *Bonsai: Best Small Stories from Aotearoa New Zealand* (Canterbury University Press, 2018) and *More Favourable Waters* (The Cuba Press, 2021). He is a landscape gardener, creative writing teacher and freelance writer.